The Depths Below

Samantha Bell

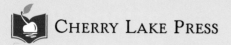

CHERRY LAKE PRESS

Published in the United States of America by Cherry Lake Publishing Group
Ann Arbor, Michigan
www.cherrylakepublishing.com

Reading Adviser: Beth Walker Gambro, MS, Ed., Reading Consultant, Yorkville, IL

Library of Congress Cataloging-in-Publication Data

Names: Bell, Samantha, author.
Title: The depths below / written by Samantha Bell.
Description: Ann Arbor, Michigan : Cherry Lake Publishing, 2023. | Series: National park adventures | Audience: Grades 4-6 | Summary: "Grab your flashlight for this trip into the darkness below. Readers will explore the deep caverns and caves that continue to fascinate visitors and reveal the wonders of life on Earth from eons ago. Part of our 21st Century Skills Library, this series introduces concepts of natural sciences and social studies centered around a sense of adventure"— Provided by publisher.
Identifiers: LCCN 2023010603 | ISBN 9781668927403 (hardcover) | ISBN 9781668928455 (paperback) | ISBN 9781668929926 (ebook) | ISBN 9781668931400 (pdf)
Subjects: LCSH: National parks and reserves—United States—Juvenile literature. | Caves—United States—Juvenile literature. | Canyons—United States—Juvenile literature.
Classification: LCC E160 .B449 2023 | DDC 917.3—dc23/eng/20230327
LC record available at https://lccn.loc.gov/2023010603

Cherry Lake Publishing Group would like to acknowledge the work of the Partnership for 21st Century Learning, a Network of Battelle for Kids. Please visit http://www.battelleforkids.org/networks/p21 for more information.

Printed in the United States of America
Corporate Graphics

Samantha Bell was born and raised near Orlando, Florida. She grew up in a family of eight kids and all kinds of pets, including goats, chickens, cats, dogs, rabbits, horses, parakeets, hamsters, guinea pigs, a monkey, a raccoon, and a coatimundi. She now lives with her family in the foothills of the Blue Ridge Mountains, where she enjoys hiking, painting, and snuggling with their cats Pocket, Pebble, and Mr. Tree-Tree Triggers.

CONTENTS

Introduction

In the national parks, visitors can explore some of the deepest places in the country. Canyons and caves showcase unique rock and lava formations. Deep waters offer beautiful scenery and unexpected surprises. There are archeological discoveries and unusual wildlife. It is no wonder thousands of people visit these sites every year.

CHAPTER 1

Grand Canyon

Grand Canyon National Park, Arizona

The Grand Canyon is a deep and massive canyon in Arizona. It stretches 277 miles (446 kilometers) long. The widest part is 18 miles (29 km) across. The whole canyon is at least 4,000 feet (1,219 meters) deep. But some parts go as deep as 6,000 feet (1,829 m). The Colorado River cuts through the bottom of the canyon. This area was first home to the Ancestral Pueblo people. They lived in the region from 200 BCE to 1110 CE. When they vanished, other Indigenous people moved in. Today, 11 Indigenous nations have connections to the land and its resources.

The Colorado River travels through the Grand Canyon.

There are more than 20 layers of rocks in the Grand Canyon.

The Grand Canyon is one of the most-studied landscapes in the world. It displays more than 20 layers of rocks. Each layer tells scientists about Earth's history. Some of the layers have ancient fossils, such as impressions of leaves and dragonfly wings. The canyon is also a land of hidden caves. Scientists estimate there are about 1,000 caves. But only 335 of them have been recorded. Most of the caves have very fragile natural and cultural resources. For example, some caves are habitats for sensitive bat species. Other caves have mineral formations, fossils, and prehistoric artifacts. For this reason, only the Cave of Domes is open to park visitors.

As the **elevation** in the canyon changes, so does the weather. The bottom of the canyon has the highest temperatures. As someone moves up the canyon, the temperature decreases. It drops 5.5 degrees Fahrenheit (15° degrees C) every 1,000 feet (305 m). The amount of **precipitation** also changes. The top of the canyon gets the most rain, while the lower parts are dry. Forests grow at the higher elevations. Some of the lower parts of the canyon are desert areas.

MORE THAN GEOLOGY

Biologists have a lot to study in the Grand Canyon, too. Habitats in the canyon include forests, deserts, streams, and rivers. These places are home to many rare and endangered animals. Only eight fish species are native to the Colorado River. Six of them are not found anywhere else in the world. The Kanab ambersnail is a small snail that is only found in two places. One of them is a large spring near the Colorado River. Other rare and endangered animals in the park include the California condor, the Mexican spotted owl, and the desert tortoise.

CHAPTER 2

Crater Lake

Crater Lake National Park, Oregon

The deepest lake in the United States is located on top of a mountain. Crater Lake sits at the top of the Cascade Mountain Range. Thousands of years ago, a 12,000-foot (3,658 m) volcano called Mount Mazama erupted. The eruption caused the mountain to collapse inward and created a large crater. Snow and rain filled the crater with water, forming Crater Lake. Eruptions continued, and a **volcanic cinder cone** formed in the crater. Today, it rises more than 750 feet (229 m) out of the lake. It is called Wizard Island. Visitors can drive around the crater on the 33-mile (53 km) Rim Road.

Wizard Island is a volcanic cinder cone in Crater Lake.
It rises more than 750 feet (229 m) out of the lake.

Crater Lake is 1,943 feet (592 m) deep. It is still filled by rain and snow. Each year, it receives approximately 43 feet (13 m) of snow. No other water sources run into the lake. This means no soil or mineral deposits run into the lake, either. Because of this, Crater Lake has some of the cleanest and clearest water in the world. Park rangers test the clarity with a special 8-inch (20 centimeters) disc. When the disc is lowered into the water, it can be seen more than 100 feet (31 m) down.

Phantom Ship Island is another island in Crater Lake.

Scientists use a Deep Rover explorer vehicle
to do aquatic moss research in Crater Lake.

For many years, scientists wondered what was at the bottom of the lake. Advances in technology have helped them find out. In 1959, they used **echo sounding machines** to map the main geological features. Then in 1988 and 1989, scientists used a Deep Rover explorer vehicle. They found mistakes in the first maps. In 2000, they mapped the floor of the lake again. This time, they used much more advanced echo sounding equipment. They collected 16 million soundings. It is the most accurate map of the bottom of the lake. The features include volcanic vents. These cracks in the lake floor spout hot water into the lake.

A SECRET GARDEN

The water in Crater Lake is very cold. On the surface, it averages around 55° Fahrenheit (12.8° C). The temperature below 300 feet (91 m) is around 38° Fahrenheit (3.3° C). One species of moss grows from about 98 feet (30 m) down to 328 feet (100 m) down. At this level, it has only about one percent of the light at the surface. Bacteria and other microorganisms live among the moss. Underneath the live moss are layers of dead moss. Scientists believe the layers may be several thousand years old.

CHAPTER 3

Mammoth Cave

Mammoth Cave National Park, Kentucky

The word *mammoth* is used to describe something huge in size. Mammoth Cave in Kentucky has earned the name. This cave is the longest known cave system in the world. So far, 426 miles (685.6 km) of the cave have been measured. The park estimates that there may be another 600 miles (966 km) in the cave system. The cave is made of limestone. It was formed by water seeping through the **crevices** of a massive rock. As the water flowed, it eroded the rock little by little. The passageways of Mammoth Cave are stacked on top of each other in five different levels. The park also has more than 200 other caves. But they are no longer connected to the cave system.

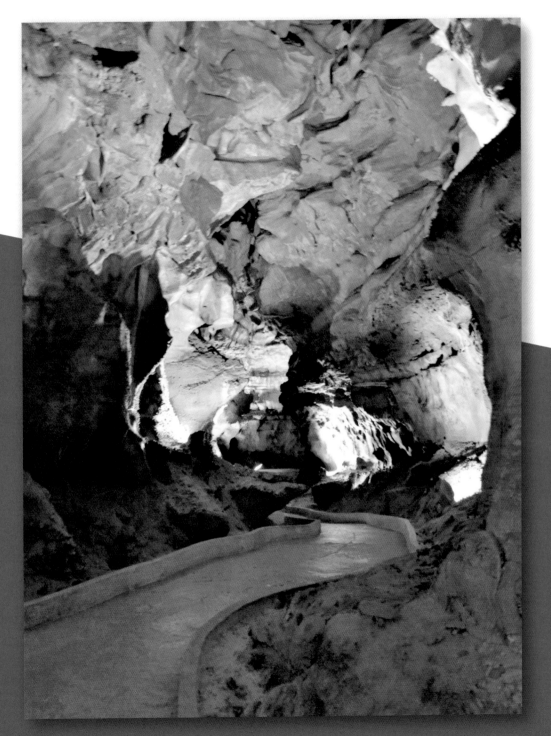

Inside Mammoth Cave in Mammoth Cave National Park, Kentucky

In this section of Mammoth Cave, visitors need to walk in a single file. It's called Black Snake Avenue.

Archeologists have found many prehistoric artifacts in the cave. They provide clues about the ancient Indigenous peoples who lived 2,000 to 4,000 years ago. These prehistoric explorers discovered more than 19 miles (31 km) of passageways in Mammoth Cave. They made torches from river cane to light their way. They used mussel shells to scrape minerals from the walls. Archeologists believe they may have used the minerals for medicine, agriculture, or trade. Prehistoric cave art can be seen along the mining routes. Many of these artifacts, including ancient sandals and bowls, can be seen in the cave today.

Wildlife is found in the cave system, too. The underground habitat is home to 130 wildlife species. Some of them live only in the cave. They have adapted to the dark environment. One of the most well-known species is the eyeless cave fish. Since it cannot see, it no longer grows eyes. The Kentucky cave shrimp does not have eyes, either. These shrimp live in the lowest cave streams. They have transparent shells that make them hard to find.

MAKING THEIR MARK

White settlers discovered Mammoth Cave around the 1790s. But it was an enslaved teenager named Stephen Bishop who paved the way for most tourists. In 1837, 17-year-old Stephen was sent into the cave to explore. He crossed caverns, sailed on underground rivers, and discovered tunnels. He became an expert guide in the cave and taught two other enslaved men, too. They used candle smoke to sign their names on the cave ceiling. Many tourists also have signed their names. The signatures are still there.

CHAPTER 4

Badwater Basin

Death Valley National Park, California and Nevada

The lowest point in North America is also the hottest and driest. Badwater Basin in Death Valley National Park is located 282 feet (86 m) below sea level. It sits between the Panamint and Black Mountain ranges. Although winters are mild, summers can be scorching. High temperatures in Death Valley have reached more than 130 degrees Fahrenheit (54˚C). Most years, the park gets only about 2.2 inches (5.6 cm) in rainfall.

The land in Badwater Basin is a salt flat.

Devils Golf Course is an area of Badwater Basin. Here, mud and hard salt have been shaped and eroded by wind and rain.

The land in Badwater Basin is known as a salt flat. Salt flats form when a body of water **evaporates** and leaves minerals and salt behind. Rain falls on the mountains surrounding Badwater Basin. The rainwater flows over the rocks and dissolves some of the minerals. The water floods Badwater Basin, forming temporary lakes. The water evaporates, and the salt and minerals cover the ground. In some places, the salt takes the shape of geometric **polygons**. Visitors can see the salt flats from their cars or from the boardwalk. During cooler months, they can walk a quarter mile (402 m) out onto the salt flats to see the salt polygons.

HOME AGAIN

Despite the area's harsh conditions, Death Valley has been the home of the Timbisha Shoshone people for thousands of years. They called their homeland Tüpippüh. In 1863, the U.S. government and the Shoshone signed a treaty to end war. It also gave the United States access to the territory. But over the years, the U.S. government took the land and pushed out the Shoshone. The Shoshone eventually received federal recognition as a tribe in 1983. But they still had no land. Finally, in 2000, a law was passed to transfer 7,500 acres (3,035 hectares) back to the tribe. This act created the first tribal reservation within a national park.

Salt and minerals are left behind when water evaporates from Badwater Basin.

There is still some water in Badwater Basin. It is too salty to drink.

Even when the lakes dry up, Badwater Basin still has water. A spring flows out of the ground to feed a small pool. The salt around the spring dissolves into the water. This makes the water too salty to drink. Some stories say an early **surveyor** brought his mule to the water for a drink. The mule refused, giving it the name "Badwater." Even though the water is so salty, some organisms live there. The Badwater snail is a tiny snail only found in Badwater Basin.

CHAPTER 5

Lechuguilla Cave and Carlsbad Caverns

Carlsbad Caverns National Park, New Mexico

Carlsbad Caverns National Park is located in the Guadalupe Mountains. The park has 120 known caves. Three of them are open to the public. The caves are made of limestone. Most limestone caves have streams, rivers, or lakes inside them. But there are no streams in the caves at Carlsbad Caverns. Geologists discovered that sulfuric acid formed these caves. The acid dissolved the rock deep underground. It created a maze of passageways of all different sizes.

Hikers walk through long tunnels of Lechuguilla Cave.

The largest and deepest cave is Lechuguilla Cave. It is 145 miles (233.4 km) long and about 1,604 feet (489 m) deep. For many years, people thought it was a small cave with dead-end passages. Then in the 1950s, cavers heard wind coming up from beneath the rubble on the cave floor. In 1984, a group of cavers got permission to begin digging. Two years later, they broke through. They found large walking passages with many mineral formations. Some of these formations can only be seen in Lechuguilla Cave. Today, the cave is open only for research and exploration.

AS DARK AS SMOKE

Native Americans have known about the caves for hundreds of years. The Mescalero Apache named the area the Home of the Bat. The Zuni Pueblo called it Bat Cave. In 1898, a teenager named John White found it, too. One day, he saw something dark moving near an opening in the ground. At first, he thought it was smoke. When he looked closer, he realized it was thousands of bats coming up from a hole in the ground. White began exploring the cave. Later, he brought tourists with him. He became one of the biggest promoters of the caverns.

Bats fly from the mouth of Carlsbad Caverns.

Carlsbad Cavern is the second-largest cave. The cavern is 30 miles (48 km) long. It has the largest cave chamber in North America. This chamber is known as the Big Room. It is approximately 4,000 feet (1,219 m) long and 625 feet (191 m) wide. It rises 255 feet (78 m) high at the tallest point. The chamber is so big it could hold six American football fields. It is full of beautiful mineral formations. Outside the cave, visitors can experience the bat flight. From late spring to fall, thousands of Brazilian free-tailed bats swarm out of the cavern. Visitors can watch them leave every evening. Or they can see them return early in the morning.

Activity

Plan Your Adventure!

Take a trip to one of the deep places in the national parks. Watch a canyon sunrise, explore a cave, or walk on salt. There are many new sights to discover and things to do. Be sure to check out the other books in the series to find out about more the national parks!

Simple Salt Flats

The salt flats discussed in chapter 4 were formed when rainwater rushing down the mountainside picked up salt and other minerals from the ground. The salty water collected in Badwater Basin. After the water evaporated, just the salt was left behind. You can try out this process for yourself. Depending on the climate where you live, it may take several days to see the final result.

Supplies:

Shallow pan

Clear glass of water

Table salt

Stirring spoon

First, add 3 to 5 spoonfuls of salt to the glass of water. Next, use the spoon to stir the water until the salt dissolves. Pour the saltwater into a shallow pan. Set the pan in a sunny area in your home. The heat from the Sun will help speed up the evaporation process. When all the water is gone from the pan, the salt will be left at the bottom of it. A similar process creates the salt flats at Badwater Basin.

Learn More

Books

Chin, Jason. *Grand Canyon.* New York, NY: Roaring Brook Press, 2017.

Felix, Rebecca. *What's Great about Oregon?* Minneapolis, MN: Lerner Classroom, 2015.

Gilbert, Sara. *Death Valley.* Mankato, MN: Creative Education, 2016.

Koontz, Robin. *Carlsbad Caverns.* Vero Beach, FL: Rourke Educational Media, 2019.

On the Web

With an adult, learn more online with these suggested searches.

"Badwater Basin." National Park Service.

"Crater Lake Photo Gallery." National Park Service.

"Fly Through Grand Canyon Animation." Grand Canyon National Park.

"Hidden Worlds: Carlsbad Caverns National Park." Harpers Ferry Center – National Park Service.

Glossary

biologists (by-AH-luh-jists) scientists who study living things

crevices (KREH-vuhss-ez) narrow openings or cracks in a rock

echo sounding machines (EH-koh SOWN-ding muh-SHEENZ) machines that calculate the depth of the water by measuring the time it takes for a signal to reach the bottom and the echo to return

elevation (eh-luh-VAY-shuhn) the height of something above sea level or ground level

evaporates (ih-VAH-puh-rayts) when a substance turns from a liquid into a gas, such as water vapor

polygons (PAH-lee-gahnz) shapes with three or more sides

precipitation (prih-sih-puh-TAY-shuhn) water falling in the form of rain, snow, sleet, or hail

surveyor (suhr-VAY-uhr) a person who measures the shape, area, and elevation of land

volcanic cinder cone (vahl-KAH-nik SIN-duhr KOHN) a small volcano that forms after a violent eruption

Index